D0520757

BY JAMES S. KELLEY
THE SOUTHWEST DIVISION
THE DALLAS MAVERICKS
THE HOUSTON ROCKETS
THE MEMPHIS GRIZZLIES
THE NEW ORLEANS HORNETS
THE SAN ANTONIO SPURS

Published in the United States of America by
The Child's World® • 1980 Lookout Drive
Mankato, MN 56003-1705
800-599-READ • www.childsworld.com

ACKNOWLEDGEMENTS

The Child's World®: Mary Berendes, Publishing Director

The Design Lab: Kathleen Petelinsek, Design and Page Production

Manuscript consulting and photo research by Shoreline Publishing Group LLC.

PHOTOS

Cover: Corbis
Interior photos: AP/Wide World: 4, 22; Corbis: 25, 28; Reuters: 7, 8, 13, 14, 16, 19, 20, 26, 31, 32

LIBRARY OF CONGRESS CATALOGING-IN-PUBLICATION DATA

Kelley, James S., 1960–

The Southwest division / by James S. Kelley.

p. cm. — (Above the rim)

Includes index.

ISBN 978-1-59296-986-9
(library bound : alk. paper)

1. National Basketball Association—History—Juvenile literature. 2. Basketball—Southwest, New—History—Juvenile literature. I. Title. II. Series.

GV885.515.N37K448 2008

796.323'640973—dc22 2007034767

CONTENTS

On the cover: In 2007, Sports Illustrated *called Tim Duncan of the San Antonio Spurs the best power forward in NBA history.*

If you want to find the best NBA team of the past decade, head Southwest. That's the home division of the San Antonio Spurs, who have won four NBA titles since 1999, the most in the league. Their victory over Cleveland in the 2007 **NBA Finals** made them as close to a dynasty as there is in pro sports these days.

The Spurs' road to the Finals, though, has never been made easy by their very tough division mates. The Dallas Mavericks have had regular 50-win teams, while the Houston Rockets are usually a balanced team. Of course, all three teams play in Texas, which makes them natural rivals. The Memphis Grizzlies and New Orleans Hornets are younger **franchises**, but improving. Read on to find out more about the Southwest Division.

CHAPTER ONE

THE DALLAS MAVERICKS

Mark Aguirre was not afraid to take it to the hoop, even against All-Star Kareem Abdul-Jabbar.

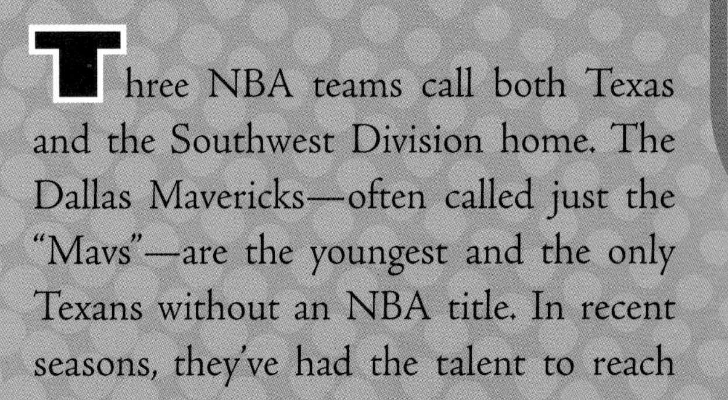

Three NBA teams call both Texas and the Southwest Division home. The Dallas Mavericks—often called just the "Mavs"—are the youngest and the only Texans without an NBA title. In recent seasons, they've had the talent to reach the top, but haven't been able to take that last leap to earn the ultimate prize.

The team started in the 1980–81 season. Coach Dick Motta, who only two years earlier had guided the Washington Bullets to an NBA title, tried everything to get this new team to win games. Once, during halftime of a game, he entered the locker room with a live tiger to scare the laziness out of his players.

Jason Kidd didn't meet expectations in Dallas, but moved on to NBA Finals' stardom with the New Jersey Nets.

Nothing worked. The Mavs finished a league-worst 15–67 in their rookie season. After that, their win totals climbed in each of the next four seasons.

In 1986–87, the Mavs rolled to a 55–27 record and won the Midwest Division (the Southwest Division was created in 2004–05). Forward Mark Aguirre and guard Rolando Blackman, both All-Stars who had arrived in Dallas as rookies in the franchise's second season, were the featured players. **Power forward** Sam Perkins was a rising star.

The next year, the Mavs won 53 games and earned another playoff run. However, that was a high point for quite a while. The Mavericks went into a tailspin for a decade. In 1992–93, Dallas won just 11 games, and it began the next season with a 1–23 record before finishing 13–69. Big "D" stood for "disaster."

In the early 1990s, Dallas used three consecutive top-10 **draft** picks to select guard Jimmy Jackson (1992), forward Jamal Mashburn (1993), and guard Jason Kidd (1994). Hailed as the "Three Js," this trio was supposed to return the Mavericks to glory. Unfortunately, the Three Js began to stand for Jealousy, Juvenile, and Jinxed. Jackson, Mashburn, and Kidd argued off the court and had trouble sharing the ball on it. The Mavericks eventually traded all three of them.

German Dirk Nowitzki has one of the best long-range shooting touches among big men.

In 1998, forward Dirk Nowitzki, just 20 years old and 7 feet tall, arrived from Germany. Nowitzki plays a nearly flawless game and has a deadly outside shot that, because of his height, is virtually unblockable. By the 2002–03 season, Nowitzki had established himself as a star, ranking in the league's top 10 in both scoring and rebounding.

Forward Michael Finley, pass-happy guard Steve Nash, and Nowitzki gave Dallas a potent offense, and Dallas became one of the league's most entertaining teams—and one of the best, too.

Mark Cuban earned his giant pile of money by selling an Internet audio company he had founded.

On the court, the two players led the team. Off the court, veteran coach Don Nelson ran the show. And over them all was the biggest new face with the Mavs—owner Mark Cuban. He had made billions in Internet businesses and loved basketball, so he bought the team. Cuban brought new energy to the team and its fans (and fancy computers to the locker room).

UP
41
MARSHALL

He sat with the fans, cheered for his team, and hired great players.

Suddenly, the Mavs were a big national story. The Mavericks won 53 regular-season games in 2000–01, 57 games in

2001–02, and a franchise-record 60 games in 2002–03. In the 2002–03 postseason, Dallas won seven-game series over both the Portland Trail Blazers and the Sacramento Kings. But the Mavericks' championship hopes ended in the conference finals, when eventual NBA champion (and division rival) San Antonio won in six games.

The best part of the Mavs' run to the 2006 NBA Finals? They beat former star Steve Nash and Phoenix to get there.

Things changed . . . Nash moved on to Phoenix, and Avery Johnson took over from Nelson. But Nowitzki remains a powerful force, and newcomers such as point guard Jason Terry and center Erick Dampier helped Dallas forge a 58–24 record in 2004–05. The Mavericks finished just one game behind the Spurs in the race for the first Southwest Division title.

They trailed the Spurs in the division again in 2005–06, but won the conference playoffs and finally earned a trip to the NBA Finals. They fell short in their quest to match their fellow Texans from San Antonio, losing to the red-hot Miami Heat. The Mavs came back in to win the division with a conference-best 67 wins in 2006–07. Nowitzki was the league MVP. However, in one of the NBA's most stunning upsets, they lost to the eighth-seeded Golden State Warriors in the first round of the playoffs.

Mavs owner Mark Cuban brought a fan's enthusiasm for running the team; he spends most games sitting with fans.

After so many near-misses, do the Mavs have what it takes to make it to the top?

CHAPTER TWO

THE HOUSTON ROCKETS

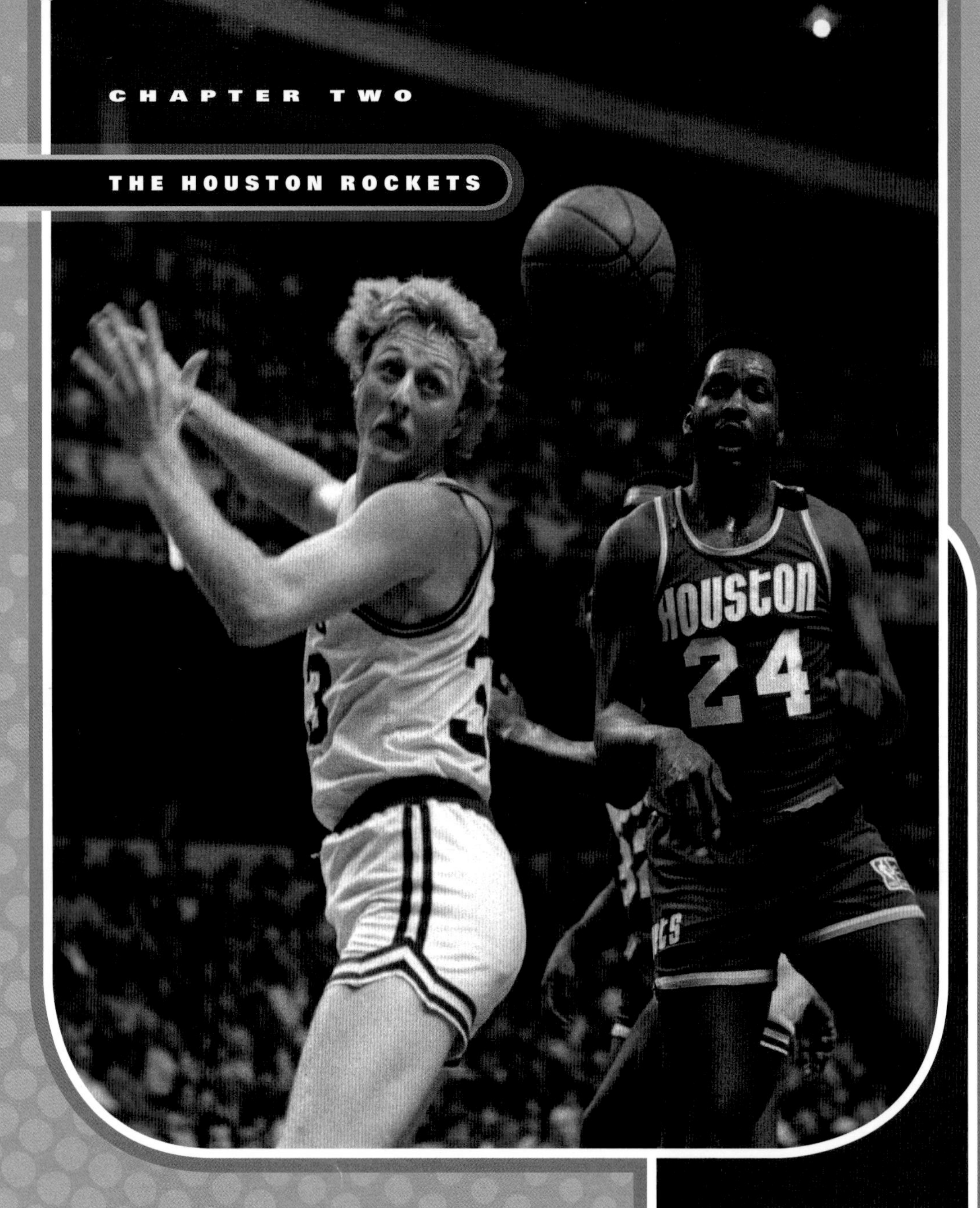

Moses Malone (24) and the Rockets reached the NBA Finals in 1981 before falling to the Boston Celtics.

Sometimes, it just takes a little while to win. That's the case for the Houston Rockets. They battled for 27 seasons, coming closer and closer to their first NBA title. Finally, they got their rings when a certain superstar guard who had foiled their plans took some time off to play . . . baseball! That's right, while Michael Jordan, who was dominating the NBA in the 1990s, went to play minor league baseball, the Rockets slipped in and won a pair of NBA titles.

The road to those two titles began in 1967 as the San Diego Rockets. (Their first draft pick that season was Pat Riley, who would go on to greater success as an NBA coach than as a player.) San Diego finished the season with the NBA's worst record, 15–67.

Calvin Murphy set a single-season NBA record in the 1980–81 season, when he made 95.8 percent of his free throws.

Rewarded with the top overall pick in the 1968 draft, San Diego chose Elvin Hayes. As a rookie, "the Big E" led the NBA in scoring (28.4 points per game) and was fourth in rebounding. Hayes, a 6-foot-10 power forward, finished in the top three in the league in both scoring and rebounding the next two seasons. Two of Hayes' teammates would become the most popular players in franchise history. Rudy Tomjanovich, a sweet-shooting 6-foot-8 forward, would later coach Houston to its championships. Calvin Murphy, a 5-foot-9 dynamo, would retire as the franchise's all-time leading scorer. Both spent their entire careers in Rockets' uniforms.

In 1981, the Rockets finished with an underwhelming 40–42 record but made it all the way to the NBA Finals. Their big man, in more ways than one, was three-time NBA MVP Moses Malone. However, the underdog Rockets lost to Boston in the Finals.

In both 1983 and 1984, the Rockets had the number-one overall picks in the NBA draft. They chose 7-foot-4 Ralph Sampson and 6-foot-10 Hakeem Olajuwon, respectively. The "Twin Towers," as the pair became known, returned the Rockets to the NBA playoffs in 1986. In the conference finals, Houston stunned the defending-champion Los Angeles Lakers. To win Game 5 of that series, Sampson made a famous off-balance **buzzer-beater**. Houston, however, once again fell to the Celtics in the finals.

Over the next decade, Olajuwon, a Nigerian native who had played soccer—not basketball—as a youth, became the league's dominant center. He was graceful and, thanks to his soccer background, blessed with extraordinary footwork in the **low post**.

In 1993–94, Olajuwon, nicknamed "the Dream," earned the league's Most Valuable Player award after leading the Rockets to a 58–24 record. In the NBA Finals, the Rockets faced the New York Knicks, who had the league's next-best center of the era, Patrick Ewing. Olajuwon dominated Ewing and the Rockets—finally—brought an NBA championship to Houston.

Nigerian-born Hakeem "The Dream" Olajuwon helped Houston "rocket" upward in the NBA.

Olajuwon was among the NBA's best centers ever. He is in the all-time top 10 in scoring, is the only center in the top 10 in steals, and is the NBA's all-time blocked shots leader.

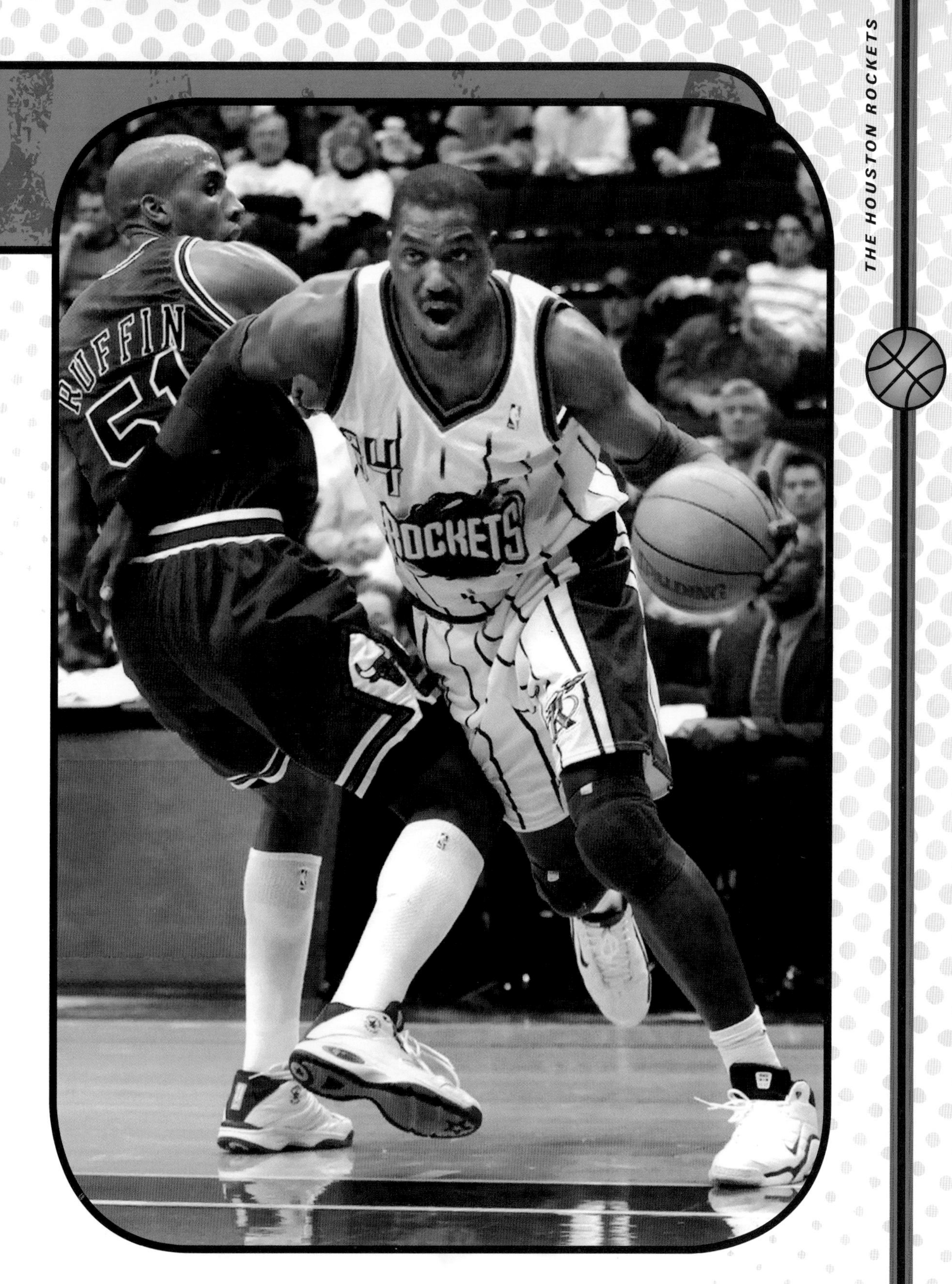
RUFFIN
ROCKETS

Tall twosome: High-scoring Tracy McGrady (left) and inside force Yao Ming give the Rockets one of the best one-two punches in the league.

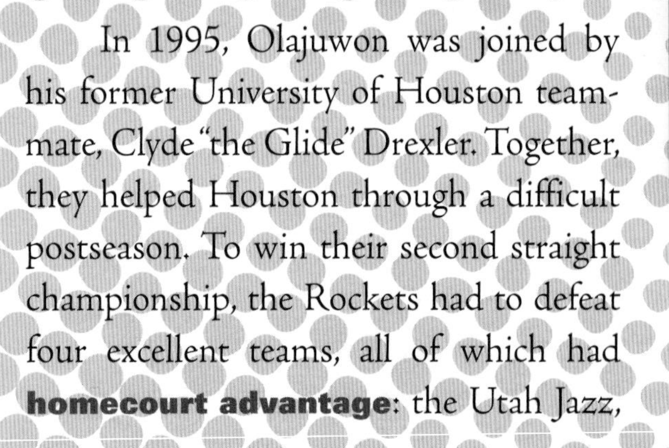

In 1995, Olajuwon was joined by his former University of Houston teammate, Clyde "the Glide" Drexler. Together, they helped Houston through a difficult postseason. To win their second straight championship, the Rockets had to defeat four excellent teams, all of which had **homecourt advantage**: the Utah Jazz,

Yao Ming was the first player from China taken with the first overall pick of the NBA Draft. He still occasionally plays for the Chinese National Team as well.

the Phoenix Suns, the San Antonio Spurs, and the Orlando Magic.

With a supporting cast that included Robert Horry, Sam Cassell, and Kenny Smith, the Rockets hung in and won. Houston faced elimination games five times, winning all five games. In the finals, with Olajuwon facing off against mighty Shaquille O'Neal, then of the Orlando Magic, the Rockets won four straight to earn their second title.

In 2002, the Rockets once again drafted a foreign-born center. Yao Ming, from China, is 7-foot-5. Yao not only has tremendous basketball skills, but also a winning personality, just like Olajuwon.

Yao joined guard Steve Francis to give the Rockets an inside-outside combination that helped the team win 45 regular-season games in 2003–04 and advance to the playoffs for the first time in five seasons. Francis was gone the next season, but high-scoring guard Tracy McGrady soon joined Yao and the Rockets, and Houston went 51–31 and made the postseason again. McGrady is one of the NBA's best all-around players and a perfect match for the inside game of Yao.

Yao and "T-Mac" have helped the Rockets make the playoffs in two of the past three seasons (through 2007), but in a tough division, the Rockets will need more jets if they want to fly back to the top.

CHAPTER THREE

THE MEMPHIS GRIZZLIES

On Vancouver's way out of town, Shareef Abdur-Rahim signed an autograph for a fan at a team goodbye party.

The Memphis Grizzlies have done a lot of moving around in their short life as a team. They joined the NBA in 1995, but were located in Vancouver, Canada. Along with the also-brand-new Toronto Raptors, they were the first NBA franchises in Canada since the Toronto

Huskies played way back in 1947. It was not a great start for the Vancouver team—their 15–67 record was the league's worst. That record included 19-game and 23-game losing streaks, and one loss to San Antonio by 49 points.

The team had some decent players. Guard Greg Anthony was the team's leading scorer at 14.0 points per game and Byron Scott was a solid outside shooter. The center was 7-foot rookie center Bryant "Big Country" Reeves. But they weren't enough.

Selecting third in the 1996 NBA draft, Vancouver chose 6-foot-9 forward Shareef Abdur-Rahim. The former University of California star had left Berkeley after becoming the first freshman in Pac-10 history to be named the conference's player of the year. He immediately became Vancouver's go-to player. He averaged 18.7 points per game in 1996–97, tops on the club. Instead of improving, though, Vancouver sank to 14–68 and again had the poorest record in the NBA.

In those early seasons, Vancouver's year-end win-loss records resembled dates on a history quiz: 15–67, 14–68, 19–63, and, in the strike-shortened 1999 season, 8–42. Abdur-Rahim did his best on poor teams. In 1998, his 22.3 points per game ranked sixth in the league.

The Toronto Huskies played for only one season in the Basketball Association of America in 1947. The BAA was one of two leagues that joined to form the NBA in 1948.

In 1998, the Grizzlies used the second pick in the draft to take Mike Bibby, a gifted point guard. In 1999, they chose shooting guard Steve Francis from the University of Maryland. Francis immediately declared that he would never play for Vancouver, which left the franchise in a tight spot. They traded Francis (who would go on to share the NBA Rookie of the Year award) to Houston and received Bibby's former University of Arizona teammate Michael Dickerson, three other players, and a future draft pick in return.

That season, 1999–2000, Vancouver finished last in the Midwest (22–60) for the fourth time in its five years. After the 2000–01 season, Bibby headed south to play for the Sacramento Kings. With attendance heading in the same direction, Vancouver decided to move the entire franchise south—to Memphis, Tennessee. Abdur-Rahim, the nearest thing to a star that the franchise had, was traded to the Atlanta Hawks.

The Memphis Grizzlies were almost an entirely new team, in an entirely new location. New general manager Jerry West shrewdly acquired a high draft pick for Abdur-Rahim, so that on draft day of 2001, Memphis had two of the first six picks. The club drafted 6-foot-10 forward Shane Battier, the national college player of the year, from Duke University.

Former Duke All-America Shane Battier, shown here blocking a shot, was a defensive ace for Memphis.

Grizzlies' general manager Jerry West was one of the NBA's all-time best guards. It is his silhouette that is used on the NBA logo.

NBA
ANDERSEN
12
MEMPHIS
31

None shall pass: Spaniard Pau Gasol (left) is not afraid to use his seven-foot body to keep opponents from making it to the basket.

The Grizzlies also acquired Pau Gasol from Spain. Gasol had been drafted by the Atlanta Hawks and then was traded to the Grizzlies.

Both Gasol and Battier were named to the All-Rookie first team. Gasol averaged 17.6 points and 8.9 rebounds per game and was the 2002 Rookie of the Year.

Slowly but surely, the Grizzlies have improved. In 2002–03, West traded for 2001 Rookie of the Year Mike Miller. Aided by the talents of point guard Jason Williams and center Stromile Swift, the 2003 Grizzlies won 28 games.

That set the stage for the best season in club history in 2003–04. With a solid core of returning players familiar with each other, Memphis won 50 games and made the playoffs for the first time in its brief history. The Grizzlies were just 17–18 in early January before reeling off a club-record eight consecutive victories to establish themselves as a postseason contender.

Mike Miller won the NBA Sixth Man Award in 2006–07.

Gasol led the team in several categories, including scoring (17.7 points per game); Miller and James Posey provided potent outside shooting; and Battier was a force on both offense and defense. West was named the league's executive of the year, and Hubie Brown was named the coach of the year.

The Grizzlies made the playoffs in 2004, 2005, and 2006. The 2005–06 season was especially memorable, as Gasol became the club's first All-Star. Though each season ended with early playoff losses, they were signs that team was headed in the right direction. It all began by migrating south and adding West.

CHAPTER FOUR

THE NEW ORLEANS HORNETS

Muggsy Bogues (left) may have been one of the smallest players in NBA history, but he had one of the biggest hearts.

New Orleans was once home to a team called the Jazz, which makes sense, as the city is known for that style of music. However, the Jazz took their show on the road to Utah in 1979, and the city was hoops-free until 2002. That's when the Hornets moved from their "hive" in Charlotte, North Carolina, to the city known as "The Big Easy." The move was a tough one for the team, but things might be looking up on the court, just as they are for the citizens of the city still dealing with the effects of 2005's Hurricane Katrina.

The Hornets first began as an **expansion team** in Charlotte in 1988, playing in a state best known for its college basketball tradition. North Carolina was known for its passionate basketball fans, who followed famous and talented local college teams such as the University of North Carolina, Duke, and Wake Forest. Many of those same fans filled the Charlotte Arena, known as the Hive, to see NBA pros play.

Larry Johnson starred in a funny series of TV commercials for which he put on a dress and played a basketball-playing character called "Grandmama."

A number of those early Hornets became fan favorites. Point guard Tyrone "Muggsy" Bogues was only 5-foot-3, but he played with tremendous energy and competitive fire. Larry Johnson was drafted out of the University of Nevada-Las Vegas in 1991. In 1992, the team added Georgetown University center Alonzo Mourning to its roster. Now the squad was complete. With Mourning's defense and rebounding setting the tone, the club made the playoffs in 1993. There they shocked the Boston Celtics, beating them in four games. The home fans went wild as Mourning's buzzer-beater sealed the victory for the Hornets.

The young team continued to grow. The Hornets made the playoffs again in 1995. In 1996, they said goodbye to Johnson and Mourning in a pair of trades that shocked and angered many fans. The team managed to win back the crowds the following season, however. New Hornets Glen Rice and Vlade Divac led the team to a franchise-record 54 victories. The Hive was buzzing again.

There were more changes to come. The team traded Bogues to Golden State in 1997. Players were saddened by the death of guard Bobby Phills in a car accident in 2000. But the biggest change of all came in 2002, when the team announced it would be moving to New Orleans for the 2002–03 season.

The former home of the NBA's New Orleans Jazz (a team that had moved to Utah) welcomed its new team with open arms. The Hornets did not disappoint, winning 47 games and remaining in the chase for the top conference seed in the playoffs until late in the season. A six-game loss to the Philadelphia 76ers in the opening round of the postseason closed out a good year on a down note.

Star forward Jamal Mashburn was hurt much of the following season, but guard Baron Davis and center Jamaal

After Hurricane Katrina hit the Gulf Coast in 2005, the Hornets played part of their schedule in Oklahoma City.

Jamal Mashburn shows off his scoring touch and fearless attitude, leaping to score over the Lakers' Robert Horry.

Magloire stepped up their games and earned All-Star spots. The Hornets made the playoffs for the seventh time in eight seasons despite finishing just 41–41.

OKC
NEW ORLEANS
16

Peja Stojakovich (PAY-zhuh Stoy-AH-kuh-vitch) was born in Yugoslavia. He recently became a citizen of Greece, however, where he moved so he could play for the national basketball team in international events.

Unfortunately, that turned out to be an indication of decline. Mashburn was traded to Philadelphia in the middle of the 2004–05 season, and the Hornets went into full rebuilding mode when Davis was shipped to Golden State at the trade deadline later in the year. New Orleans slumped to just 18 wins and finished in last place in the Southwest Division's first year.

From 2005–2007, however, the team improved each year and missed the 2007 NBA playoffs by just three games. In 2006–07, the Hornets showed balance in their lineup, as six regulars averaged at least 10 points per game. Star forward Peja Stojakovic was one of them, but missed much of the season due to injury. Had he been healthy, the Hornets might have returned to the playoffs. As it was, David West led the team with an average of 17.3 points per game.

Though Peja Stojakovich has one of the NBA's best outside shooting touches, he's not afraid to "take it to the hoop," as well.

CHAPTER FIVE

THE SAN ANTONIO SPURS

Few players in league history scored as many points with as much grace and style as George "The Iceman" Gervin.

As long as Tim Duncan is around, the road to the NBA title goes through San Antonio, Texas. He has led the Spurs to four NBA titles in nine years, with the most recent coming in the 2006–07 season.

Only Michael Jordan (10) and Wilt Chamberlain (7) have led the NBA in scoring in more seasons than George Gervin (4).

But while the most recent decade has brought a quartet of NBA titles, earlier seasons brought success to San Antonio, too. Since joining the NBA prior to the 1976–77 season, the Spurs have consistently been a winning franchise.

However, the history of the team goes farther back than that. The Spurs actually began play in 1967 as the Dallas Chaparrals of the American Basketball Association (ABA). The franchise moved to San Antonio in 1973 and was renamed the Spurs.

In 1976, San Antonio became one of four teams from the ABA to join the NBA when those two leagues decided to combine.

The team's big star was silky-smooth, 6-foot-8 shooter George Gervin. "The Iceman," as he was known, was an incredible scoring machine. With his patented **finger-roll** and deadly jumper, the Iceman led the league in scoring in four different seasons. He once scored 63 points on the final day of one season to win a scoring title by less than .10 point per game. His most prolific scoring season was 1979–80, when he averaged 33.1 points per game.

The team won three consecutive Midwest Division titles from 1981–83 (the Southwest Division was started in 2004). Gervin's scoring, however, paled against the many weapons of the Los Angeles Lakers, who routed San Antonio in the Western Conference finals in both 1982 and 1983.

In 1987, San Antonio, picking first in the NBA draft for the very first time, selected 7-foot center David Robinson from the United States Naval Academy. The Spurs had to wait for "the Admiral" to finish two years in the Navy before he could join the league.

Why did David Robinson have to go into the Navy? Students at the Naval Academy are required to serve in the military right after their college years are over. There are no exceptions—even for star athletes.

In 1989, Robinson started play, along with forward Sean Elliott. Two of the league's best community leaders off the court, as well as All-Stars on it, Robinson and Elliott reversed the franchise's course. San Antonio went from 21 wins the previous season to 56 the next. The 35-victory leap was an NBA record. The Admiral was a shoo-in for Rookie of the Year. The next year, he won the MVP award as the Spurs posted a league-best 62 wins.

The Admiral got a new crew in 1998, when the Spurs added 7-foot rookie Tim Duncan, a native of the U.S. Virgin Islands. Blessed with a graceful bank shot and a calm manner, Duncan teamed with Robinson and Elliott to give San Antonio an excellent **frontcourt**.

Duncan won the Rookie of the Year award in 1998 and then the league MVP award in 2002 and 2003. In 1998–99, Duncan was among the league leaders in scoring and rebounding as San Antonio won its first NBA championship.

Two champs: Tim Duncan (left) holds up his NBA Finals MVP award, while David Robinson (right) shows off the Spurs' 2003 NBA championship trophy.

SPURS
21
SPURS
50

In 2002–03, Robinson's last season, San Antonio won its second title. On the way, the Spurs defeated the three-time defending champion Lakers. In the finals, they downed the New Jersey Nets, four games to two.

Tricky guard Tony Parker, a native of France, said "Merci!" ("Thanks!") to winning the 2007 NBA Finals MVP award.

With the Admiral retired, the franchise's fortunes fell squarely on Duncan's shoulders, and the big man has proved to be more than capable. In 2004–05, San Antonio went 59–23 during the regular season and edged Dallas by a single game to win the first Southwest Division crown. Duncan got help from guards Tony Parker, a native of France, and acrobatic Manu Ginobili, an import from Argentina.

The Spurs returned to the NBA Finals for the third time, this time facing the Detroit Pistons. Duncan scored 25 points and pulled down 11 rebounds in Game 7, a hard-fought 81–74 triumph, and was named the Finals MVP.

After missing the Finals in 2006, the Spurs returned to what was becoming familiar territory in 2007. In the Finals that year, they took on the Cleveland Cavaliers, led by superstar LeBron James. But not even King James was enough to defeat the all-around play of the Spurs, who won their fourth title in nine seasons with a convincing sweep. Parker was named the NBA Finals MVP by averaging 24 points in the four games.

Before joining the NBA, Manu Ginobili was a two-time MVP in the Italian pro league. He has also helped Argentina win several big international tournaments.

The Spurs have great talent, but they owe their success to team play. Rather than worrying about their point totals, they work together to do whatever it takes to win. That attitude will surely "spur" them to continued success.

TIME LINE

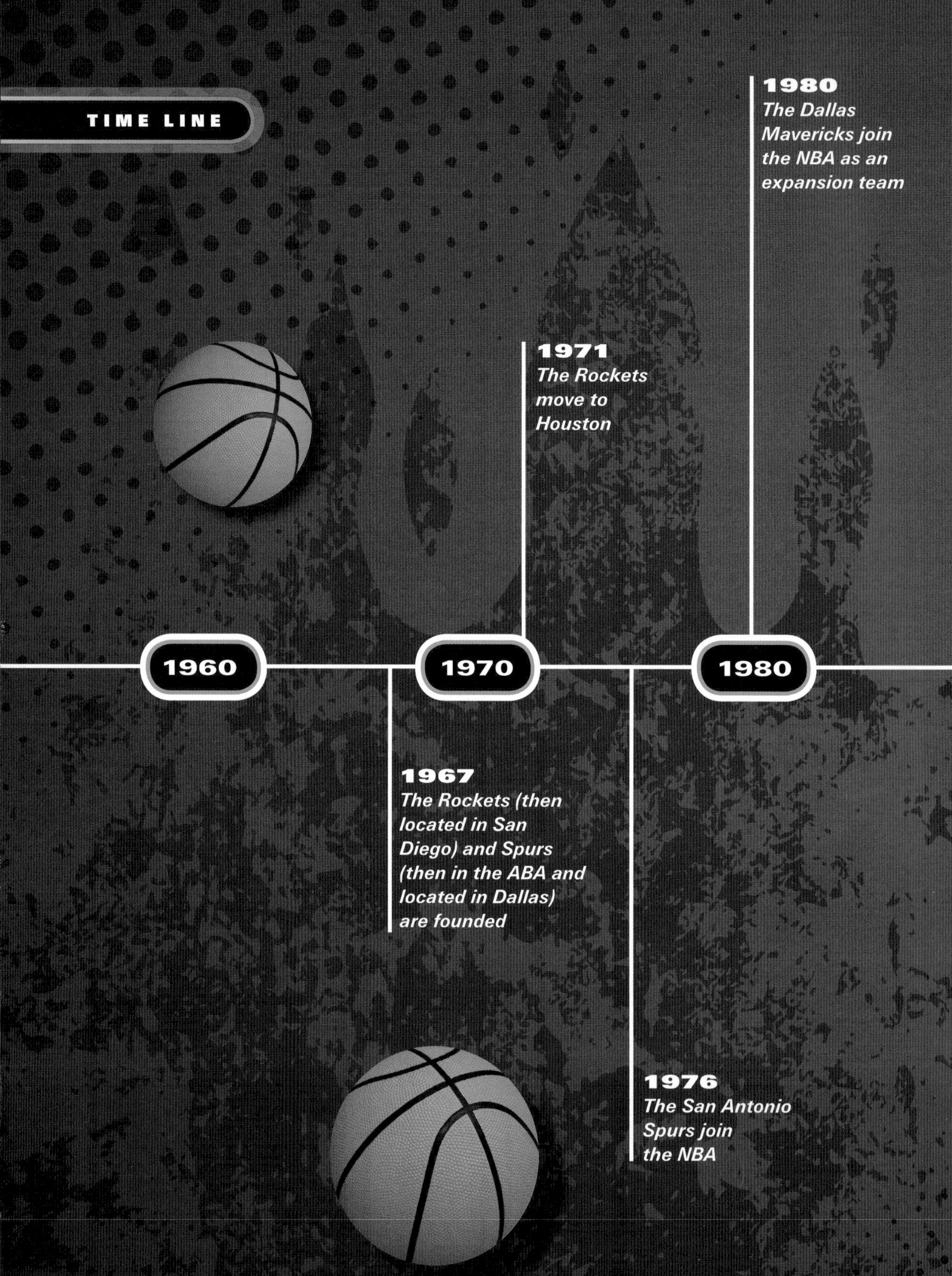

1960
1970
1980
1967
The Rockets (then located in San Diego) and Spurs (then in the ABA and located in Dallas) are founded
1971
The Rockets move to Houston
1976
The San Antonio Spurs join the NBA
1980
The Dallas Mavericks join the NBA as an expansion team

1988
The Hornets begin play as an expansion team in Charlotte

1990

1994
The Houston Rockets win the first of back-to-back NBA championships

1995
The Memphis Grizzlies are founded as the Vancouver Grizzlies

1999
San Antonio captures the NBA title

2000

2001
The Grizzlies move to Memphis

2002
The Hornets move to New Orleans

2003
San Antonio wins its second NBA championship

2004
The Grizzlies post a winning record and make the playoffs for the first time

2005
The Spurs win the NBA title for the second time in three years and the third time overall

2007
The Spurs win it all again for their fourth NBA title in nine years

2010

TEAM RECORDS
(through 2006–07)

TEAM	ALL-TIME RECORD	NBA TITLES (MOST RECENT)	NUMBER OF TIMES IN PLAYOFFS	TOP COACH (WINS)
Dallas	1,051–1,131	0	13	Don Nelson (339)
Houston	1,629–1,619	2 (1994–95)	24	Rudy Tomjanovich (503)
Memphis	318–634	0	3	Mike Fratello (95)
New Orleans	725–801	0	9	Paul Silas (208)
*San Antonio	1,871–1,383	4 (2006–07)	35	Gregg Popovich (576)

*includes ABA

MEMBERS OF THE NAISMITH MEMORIAL NATIONAL BASKETBALL HALL OF FAME

DALLAS

PLAYER	POSITION	DATE INDUCTED
Alex English	Forward	1997

HOUSTON

PLAYER	POSITION	DATE INDUCTED
Charles Barkley	Forward	2006
Rick Barry	Guard	1987
Clyde Drexler	Guard	2004
Alex Hannum	Coach	1998
Elvin Hayes	Forward/Center	1990
Moses Malone	Forward/Center	2001
Calvin Murphy	Guard	1993

SOUTHWEST DIVISION CAREER LEADERS
(through 2006–07)

TEAM	CATEGORY	NAME (YEARS WITH TEAM)	TOTAL
Dallas	Points	Rolando Blackman (1981–92)	16,643
	Rebounds	James Donaldson (1985–92)	4,589
Houston	Points	Hakeem Olajuwon (1984–2001)	26,511
	Rebounds	Hakeem Olajuwon (1984–2001)	13,382
Memphis	Points	Shareef Abdur-Rahim (1996–2001)	7,801
	Rebounds	Shareef Abdur-Rahim (1996–2001)	3,070
New Orleans	Points	Dell Curry (1988–98)	9,839
	Rebounds	Larry Johnson (1991–95)	3,479
San Antonio	Points	David Robinson (1989–2003)	20,790
	Rebounds	David Robinson (1989–2003)	10,497

MEMPHIS

PLAYER	POSITION	DATE INDUCTED
Hubie Brown	Contributor	2005

SAN ANTONIO

PLAYER	POSITION	DATE INDUCTED
George Gervin	Forward	1996
Moses Malone	Center	2001
Dominique Wilkins	Forward-Guard	2006

NEW ORLEANS

PLAYER	POSITION	DATE INDUCTED
Robert Parish	Center	2003

buzzer-beater—a shot that wins a game just as the game-ending buzzer sounds

draft—an annual selection of college players by a pro sports league

expansion team—in sports, this means a team created from scratch and added to a league

finger-roll—a type of shot made close to the basket in which the player reaches high over his head and rolls the ball off his fingertips into the basket

franchises—more than just the teams, they are the entire organizations that are members of a professional sports league

frontcourt—in this instance, a term for the forwards and center in a team's lineup; it also refers to the area on a basketball court from the centerline to the baseline on the side of the court that a team is shooting

homecourt advantage—what a team has when it will play more games in a playoff series at its home arena; most teams have greater success playing in front of their home fans

low post—the area beneath and around the basket, where taller players do most of their work

NBA Finals—a seven-game series between the winners of the NBA's Eastern and Western Conference championships

power forward—a tall, strong player who is depended upon for scoring and rebounding

sixth man—a basketball team's key substitute, the first player off the bench after the starting five

FOR MORE INFORMATION ABOUT THE SOUTHWEST DIVISION AND THE NBA

Books

Gilbert, Sara. *The Story of the Memphis Grizzlies.* Mankato, Minn.: Creative Education, 2006.

Gilbert, Sara. *The Story of the New Orleans Hornets.* Mankato, Minn.: Creative Education, 2006.

Hareas, John. *Basketball.* New York: DK Publishers, 2005.

Leboutillier, Nate. *The Story of the Houston Rockets.* Mankato, Minn.: Creative Education, 2006.

Leboutillier, Nate. *The Story of the San Antonio Spurs.* Mankato, Minn.: Creative Education, 2006.

Roselius, J Chris. *Tim Duncan: Champion On and Off the Court.* Berkeley Heights, N.J.: Enslow Publishers, 2005.

Stewart, Mark and Zeysing, Matt. *The Dallas Mavericks.* Chicago: Norwood House Press, 2006.

Young, Jeff C. *Yao Ming: Basketball's Big Man.* Berkeley Heights, N.J.: Enslow Publishers, 2005.

Zuehlke, Jeffrey. *Dirk Nowitzki (Amazing Athletes).* Minneapolis: First Avenue Editions, 2007.

On the Web

Visit our Web page for lots of links about the Southwest Division teams: *http://www.childsworld.com/links*

NOTE TO PARENTS, TEACHERS, AND LIBRARIANS: We routinely verify our Web links to make sure they are safe, active sites—so encourage your readers to check them out!

INDEX

ABOUT THE AUTHORS

James S. Kelley is the pseudonym for a group of veteran sportswriters who collaborated on this series. Among them, they have worked for *Sports Illustrated*, the National Football League, and NBC Sports. They have written more than a dozen other books for young readers on a wide variety of sports.